WAYS TO BEG

WAYS to BEG

TJ SANDELLA

BLACK LAWRENCE PRESS

Black
Lawrence
Press

www.blacklawrence.com

Executive Editor: Diane Goettel
Book and Cover Design: Zoe Norvell
Cover Art: "The Boy And The Owl" by Igor Skaletsky

Lucille Clifton, "dying" from The Collected Poems of Lucille Clifton. Copyright
© 2004 by Lucille Clifton. Reprinted with the permission of The Permissions Company,
LLC on behalf of BOA Editions, Ltd., boaeditions.org.
Tony Hoagland, excerpt from "At the Galleria" from Unincorporated Persons in the Late
Honda Dynasty. Originally from Poetry (July/August 2009). Copyright © 2009, 2010
by Tony Hoagland. Reprinted with the permission of The Permissions Company, LLC
on behalf of Graywolf Press, graywolfpress.org.

for my mom

TABLE OF CONTENTS

II.

ACKNOWLEDGMENTS

Gratitude to the editors of the following publications in which poems from this collection first appeared, often in earlier versions:

Asheville Poetry Review: "Flight"
Best New Poets: "Kayaking, Early Morning"
The Chattahoochee Review: "Communion"
Cider Press Review: "Revelation"
Cold Mountain Review: "Post-Racial"
The Comstock Review: "H(om)e"
Connotation Press: "A Lesson in Annihilation"
The Fourth River: "Diptych"
The Good Men Project: "Baptism," "*Happy #CincoDeMayo! The best taco bowls are made in Trump Tower Grill. I love Hispanics!*" and "*It's like in golf...*"
Hawai`i Pacific Review: "Psalm I"
Hiram Poetry Review: "Distractions"
Hotel Amerika: "Arrival"
New Ohio Review: "Lucy's" and "Nightmare on Elm Street"
Painted Bride Quarterly: "Abracadabra"
Passages North: "My Mother Prepares Me for Her Death"
Poet Lore: "Apartment B"
Poetry Northwest: "*Donald J. Trump is calling for a total and complete shutdown of Muslims entering the United States*"
Potomac Review: "Asylum Pastoral" and "Found Mantra in the Frozen Food Aisle"
The Rupture (formerly *The Collagist*): "Pathology of Violence"
The South Carolina Review: "After Driving Behind a Truck with a 'Redneck Romeo' Bumper Sticker" and "Nocturne Interrupted"
Spoon River Poetry Review: "Seasons"
The Tusculum Review: "Foreshadow"
Zone 3: "Kayaking, Early Morning" and "Loss"

~

"My Mother Prepares Me for Her Death" was selected by Aimee Nezhukumatathil for an Elinor Benedict Poetry Prize.

"Flight" was selected by Billy Collins for a William Matthews Poetry Prize.

"Diptych" and "Seasons" were each awarded Academy of American Poets Prizes, selected by Judson Mitcham and Kenneth Hart.

"Kayaking, Early Morning" was selected by Dorianne Laux for inclusion in the *Best New Poets* anthology.

"*Donald J. Trump is calling for a total and complete shutdown of Muslims entering the United States*" was reprinted as the *Vandal Poem of Day*.

"Diptych" was reprinted in *The Best of the Fourth River*.

Many, many thanks to Diane Goettel and everyone at Black Lawrence Press; Jad Adkins—sometime writing partner, all-the-time dude—for giving this thing a careful, thoughtful look; teachers, students, and friends of Walsh U and the Georgia College MFA program, especially Evan Allgood, Roger Sollenberger, Alice Friman, Marty Lammon, Rachel Davis, Karen McElmurray, Melissa Borries, Laura Newbern, Ron Scott, Lou Suarez, John Kandl, and Neil Carpathios.

Appreciation to the wizard, Igor Skaletsky, for lending his collage to the cover and to designer extraordinaire, Zoe Norvell, for putting it all together.

Thank you, Bob Hicok. Thank you, Jan Beatty. Thank you, Dorianne Laux. Thank you, Vaughan Ashlie Fielder and The Field Office.

Much love and gratitude to the fam: Shug, Steve, Aria, Nico, Luca, and, especially, the big guy, Papa T. And to Hannah Larter, who somehow spends every day lugging around her big ol' heart—
thank you.

ARRIVAL

It could be true—

someone crafted us out of clay, wrenched man's rib
    and named the sharp bone
wife. Maybe we were culled from ether, sprung
from the skull of a higher power, or maybe the gods sat back
bemused or aghast

as we slid and slurped our way out of the primordial ooze
and into our skin—byproducts of the big bang that bore us,

but born nonetheless.

If we arrive in our bodies
from somewhere else, then maybe there is
a *somewhere else*,

and in that misty city
our pre-life kin roam like buffalo
in search of our scent, despondent,

pawing at empty patches of us-shaped sky. Brothers, sisters,
I want the truth, not this thunder

like a telephone ringing
in the middle of the night, like an absentee father breathing heavy
on the other end of the line, *Hello? Are you out there?*

Only an answer could convince me
of a more honest prayer. And if I were to say
we tore away—fled our creator on lightning bolts
we rode bareback out of the cosmos—who could argue? In this version,

imagine those stallions bucked
and tossed their sparkling manes, but we wrapped our arms
    around their necks
and kicked our heels into their ribs. We broke them.

    We took the leap,

and out of all the possible destinations, the infinite iterations
of inhospitable planets in the vast unfathomable multiverse,

we landed softly here
among raindrops, among mountaintops. Reader,
the earth has been so generous

and the crop of questions
is in surplus. Would we be happier if we let them die on the vine
and shrivel in the sun? If we plowed them under?

Or are we destined to harvest? To sow every spring?

Do we never stop asking?

I

~

As the gods in olden stories
turned mortals into laurel trees and crows
        to teach them some kind of lesson,

so we were turned into Americans
to learn something about loneliness.

—TONY HOAGLAND

ABRACADABRA

Think of Harry Houdini in a straitjacket,
strung up by his ankles, dangling six stories
above a busy city street. Or close your eyes,
hold your breath, and think of him blindfolded and bound
in the belly of a Chinese Water Torture Cell.
He wanted to be an actor, you know,
and all those performances he perfected
were only ever meant to be a stepping-stone
to the silver screen. Did he call it failure—
having spent more time wrapped up in chains
than in the arms of a leading lady? Did he suffer—
knowing he'd settled for a lesser version
of the story he'd imagined?

In one of his most
popular acts—it could hardly be called a trick—
The Great Houdini claimed
he could withstand any blow, and night after night
men lined up to take their shots. He was buried alive
three times, but it was a jab from a seventeen-year-old kid
that killed him. I'm asking you to think
of his ruptured appendix, his organ leaking blood
like milk from a cracked glass.

Tonight, I hope you have someone
you love, but I hope that person is on a business trip
to North Dakota or the moon or at least picking up bread
from the grocery store. For now, it's just you and me
and we don't have to whisper these questions.
How many blows can we take? How many
sacrifices can we make?

And if we want more
than this bubble of escape—a few soundless minutes
underwater, our loved ones
stuck in traffic—then how long before we attempt
those truly desperate, death-defying feats? How long
until we become what we've always wanted to be?

104.7 FM, THE ZOO

Playing the best
of the '70s '80s and '90s
Mark Johnson
guided Ashtabula Ohio
through the decades
with baritone cool
spun the hits
but also advised
where to buy
deli meat
how to restructure
mortgages
which roads
had potholes

for us kids
who hadn't yet discovered
gangster rap or death metal
and still listened
to our parents' presets
he was something like a god
like Molly Ringwald
or the Goo Goo Dolls

for all we knew
they all lived in the same city
a gated community
we'd never enter
except via speaker or screen
or prayer

but on Career Day
at Aces Elementary School
in the spring of 1999
something akin to a miracle
when our principal announced
Mark would be presenting next
on the topic of *pursuing your dreams*

and even Mrs. B
the shriveled surly librarian
whose greatest joy was doling out detentions
Mrs. B who we called *Mrs. B-Word*
even she went wild
when Mark kicked open
the gymnasium doors
to an explosion of pyrotechnics
and a swarm of screaming pre-teens
of which the boys promptly sprouted
whiskers above their upper lips
and the girls sobbed and swooned
like soap opera stars
as I remember it
in the part of my brain
that will always be 11 years old

but when the smoke cleared
and his silhouette solidified
into something incongruent
with our imaginations
we were forced to recalibrate
to calculate on fingers
using the math we swore we'd never use
when we got older
to determine if Mark was an adult
like the adults we knew
or like the ones on TV and the radio

ponytail minus potbelly
divided by tube socks and sandals
times Lynyrd Skynyrd tee
to the power of sunglasses
still on against the glare
of the overhead lights

it added up
if barely
he was not our fathers or uncles
even if he was not
Kurt Cobain
or Brad Pitt

and when he closed his speech
by giving us the devil horns
and saying
go forth and rock 'n' roll
he silenced all doubts
affirmed he was indeed
from the land of celebrities
and so students lined up
to have him autograph
notebook paper and backpacks
which he did as if it were something
he was often asked to do
as if yes
his dreams had come true

and even though I recognized Mark
the moment he took the mic
as the dude
that lived around the corner from me
still with his dad
Mark who refused to wave
or smile at neighbors

when he mowed the lawn
or retrieved the mail
sunglasses always on
but like in a creepy way
his crummy Corolla parked in the driveway
every Friday and Saturday night
the mournful blue light of his TV
glowing in the dead-end dark
Mark who I long suspected
to be the saddest human being
on Walnut Boulevard
or maybe even
in all of northeast Ohio

even though I recognized
DJ Mark Johnson
as neighbor Mark Johnson
I kept quiet
afraid of ruining my friends' fun
or more likely
afraid of being called a liar
or worse

I got in line
with my pen and paper
and suspicions
I went on
and go on
as I always have
trying to pretend
that I do not know
what I think I know.

AFTER DRIVING BEHIND A TRUCK WITH A "REDNECK ROMEO" BUMPER STICKER

What would he say as he gazed through the window
    of her double-wide
after hopping the barbwire fence at the Capulet's trailer park? *O,*

she doth teach the Marlboros to blaze bright! It seems she burns
upon the breast of night. And how tenderly the lady ashes

into an empty beer! My heart is the grass, and Juliet
the John Deere! And if they locked eyes at the Capulet's hoedown,

would he think to himself, *Did my heart love 'til now?*
    Never have I seen such beauty
wrestle a wild hog to the ground. Would he woo her away from Paris
    with a country tune

about blushing bumpkins? Or prove his love
    by tattooing her name on his neck
to cover up Rosaline's? Would he watch, helpless, as Tybalt
    ran down Mercutio

in the streets of fair Verona? And give chase in his battered pickup,
    a Confederate flag
flapping from the bent antenna? Would Romeo OD on oxy?
    Could Juliet live

without her Romeo? Would their story
be of lesser woe?

DISTRACTIONS

Andiamo, she says,
because I'm still mostly dressed,
and she's been waiting over an hour

for me to find her like this—topless,
speaking in tongues—but even before
I shed my shirt or socks, I already begin to fumble

with metaphors
that may or may not land in this poem,
like the one where I compare her breasts to the two tablets

Moses dragged down from Mount Sinai,
being, as it is, that they're both, quite literally, a pair
and held firmly chest high, but, more importantly,
        that they inspire awe,

sent to us directly from god, or so a certain kind of man
might believe, willing to devote his entire life to abide by them,
teaching posterity to worship them, and it takes me
        a full few minutes

before I realize that, of course, magnificent breasts should never,
under any circumstance, be compared to old stones,
        and the religious stuff,
I see now, is a little much, and maybe, quite possibly,
        I'm a shitty poet after all,

which is precisely when she reaches over
and unfastens the belt, the button, the zipper, then tugs off
my jeans and tosses them against the wall, where they float
        momentarily

before crumpling to the floor.
Don't get the wrong idea. I've been waiting for her, too,
but I want to get this right—which is why, even when she starts

to tremble, I sometimes stall
by thinking about baseball—the fate
of middle relievers and flesh-and-blood umpires,

small-market teams and steroid cheats,
sabermetrics and the slowing speed of the game:
instant replay, lefty-righty switches, the fastidious emphasis

on each pitch—the time it takes
to do something well. And if all that imagery—
wooden bats, balls disappearing into mitts—gets too phallic,

too yonic, there's always Sister Susannah,
the leather-faced nun from Sunday school
who I could enter into one of a thousand scenarios

that could slow and soften a stallion.
But if even she somehow fails to weaken my resolve,
I'll dredge the dreary depths of childhood trauma: staying

with my aunt and uncle, up early
to watch Saturday morning cartoons, finding them
in the kitchen in all their carnal, middle-aged glory.

One could ruin an otherwise perfect evening
this way, and maybe I would,
but here she is,

pulling my face to hers—*Andiamo*,
she whispers, and this time I know
she means she's ready,

means for me to stop being the man
thinking of everything

but this.

LUCY'S

I confused guacamole
with guano
until I was seventeen
when my girlfriend's mom
patiently explained the difference
plopping a dollop onto my plate
next to the Spanish rice
catapulting me
on the long flight
from meat and potatoes
to masala and paneer
for the first time
as a freshman in college
tartare and foie gras
as a grad student
and so it goes
the older I get
the farther I travel
with my tongue
curries and compotes
caraway and cardamom
ginger and jasmine
and planes and trains
to aromatic rooms
in cities I can taste
better than I can pronounce

which have all led me here
30 years old
an orphan
more or less
alone in the corner of Cleveland's

only Ethiopian restaurant
named after the 3.2 million-year-old fossil
unearthed in the Awash Valley
an animal that roamed Africa
long before it was Africa
with the skull of an ape
and the gait of a human
bipedal bones paleontologists celebrated
as evolution's missing link
and named Lucy
after The Beatles' song that played
as they dusted and chiseled
and called deans and spouses

Lucy's Bar and Restaurant
named after a fossil
named after Lennon's psychotropic fever dream
time collapses on itself
here in Old Brooklyn
a beat-down neighborhood
on the outskirts of the city
that watched steel production
move to China in the '90s
as poverty blazed through the Midwest
condemning homes
and shuttering storefronts
but amazingly
Lucy's Bar and Restaurant survives
you can go there
and listen to the grease-stained regulars
holdovers from the location's
previous incarnation
as the working-class watering hole
and the drinks are still cheap
and you must walk through a cloud of smoke
to find a barstool

where I sit and shovel spicy shiro
with injera
a spongey slightly sour bread
served with every meal
like pita or naan
used to transport food from plate to mouth
in lieu of silverware
my oily fingers
wrapped around a Rolling Rock
to extinguish the heat
before I move on to the other samplings
on the vegetarian platter
which I've been thinking about all week
big enough for two
but I intend to eat
every last morsel
my indulgence for surviving
another five days at a desk
in an office an hour away
from the town where I was born

how far we must wander
from ourselves and our parents
and then back
to discover what we really love
to unlearn the fork and knife
and spoon and eat with our hands
the legumes and spices
that gave birth to all else
paprikash and power lines
psalms and spaghetti
marriage and meatloaf and me
and the dim smoky corners
of my body
where I can still sometimes feel
my mother and father

and all of my ancestors
and I think they're laughing
and singing
as they pass a plate
huddled together
around a fire
over which I warm my hands
thousands of years later
though I am alone
at Lucy's Bar and Restaurant
eating a meal
meant for two.

H(OM)E

Say *home* ten times fast
and it starts to sound like *Om*,
sacred, syrupy syllable
with its single claw
in every word, purred

from ascetics' mouths
until it scrambles
their brains. Say it for days,
for months, for years,
they claim,
and you can see god
in a bird, god
in a flower.

Home, too, is a matter
of repetition: these walls,
these roads, this burning
river. Cleveland,

I tried
to make a memory of you—
thought I'd find some place
I wouldn't want to leave,
with ocean views
or mountain streams,
but everywhere new
can be ruined, too,

can taste the blood
and rust on its tongue
and spit you back out

to where you're from.
City, every time
I crawl back,
it seems it's into a winter
that won't end,

so what a surprise
to be surprised,

when the snow
finally subsides
and we're again sanctified
by sunshine and skin,
both of which warm the bed
I find myself in.

Friends, if anything
could keep me here,
it's the long runway
of her back,
the river of her throat,
her highway thighs.

Heart, let any old sound
echo in your chambers.
Let me worship stupidly
this bird, that flower.

O Moon, tell me
how many people
have looked up at you
and thought,
I want to go home,

and never could,
never did.

DONALD J. TRUMP IS CALLING FOR A TOTAL AND COMPLETE SHUTDOWN OF MUSLIMS ENTERING THE UNITED STATES

—said in the third person

The number of Americans
killed annually by
jihadist immigrants 2
armed toddlers 21
lightning 39
lawnmowers 64
falling out of bed 737
total and complete
shutdown why stop
with Muslims
ban babies lightning
lawnmowers beds
send them back
to where they came from
lie down
in the tall grass
no fear of falling
no middle-of-the-night
patter of feet no child
sliding between the sheets
squeezing between you
and the nothingness
you sleep next to
lie down in the tall grass
listen to the thunder
watch lightning's
absence course

through the clouds
the dark sky
darkening.

IT'S LIKE IN GOLF. A LOT OF PEOPLE—
I DON'T WANT THIS TO SOUND TRIVIAL—
BUT A LOT OF PEOPLE ARE SWITCHING
TO THESE REALLY LONG PUTTERS. VERY
UNATTRACTIVE. IT'S WEIRD. YOU SEE
THESE GREAT PLAYERS WITH THESE
REALLY LONG PUTTERS BECAUSE THEY
CAN'T SINK THREE-FOOTERS ANYMORE.
AND I HATE IT. I'M A TRADITIONALIST.
I HAVE SO MANY FABULOUS FRIENDS
WHO HAPPEN TO BE GAY, BUT I'M A
TRADITIONALIST.

—Former President Donald J. Trump

No
it's like in basketball
you see these towering centers
who can slam it down
over the entire opposing team
their mamas papas
and all their friends nobody can stop
the behemoth's stutter-step and rise
to the rack except to chop
a forearm grab a shoulder
hold on for dear life send them
to the free-throw line
where some of the biggest baddest
bruisers turn sheepish the ball
suddenly awkward in their palms
a couple nervous dribbles bowed

knees cockeyed elbows nightmares
of air ball chants and not-top-tens
boo birds and snickering teammates
though there's an easy
and proven remedy
the granny shot
named for the feeble
effeminate mechanics a little crouch
the ball lowered between the legs
then gifted underhand
toward the hoop Hall of Famer
Wilt Chamberlain notorious
for his monster jams sweet baby hook
and foul line jitters
switched to the granny in 1962
his third year in the league upped
his free-throw percentage
from 40 to 61 percent
bagged the greatest game
of all time 100 points
against the New York Knicks
sank 28 of 32 from the line then shockingly
abandoned the granny the following year
tired of *looking like a sissy*
though his percentage plummeted to 38 percent
forget the stats
for one season a man discovered
his brilliance by doing what came naturally
gently delivering the ball from his giant hands
into its graceful arc
all eyes watching as it soared
slowly through the air
and then the satisfying swish
as it fell softly into the net
like any pair of gratified lovers
into their bed.

*HAPPY #CINCODEMAYO! THE BEST TACO
BOWLS ARE MADE IN TRUMP TOWER
GRILL. I LOVE HISPANICS!*

—Former President Donald J. Trump, via Twitter

In occupied cities Nazis commandeered farms and butcher shops first
in the 'burbs organic grass-fed everything in the 'hood organic grass-
fed nothing but fast-food chains peddling diabetes and heart disease in
colonial Massachusetts wardens scrubbed lobster from menus deemed
the present-day delicacy cruel and unusual punishment oversized bugs
bottom feeders the brief history of our species marred by fetid feasts
scorched earth salted fields and one time I ordered vegetarian chili
from a bar in Cleveland Ohio and a man a few stools down rolled
his eyes shook his head and mumbled *pussy* into his Miller Lite so
we know food is political the taco bowl an emblem of American
efficiency eight-hour workdays rice assembly lines appropriation
seasoned beef Frida Diego sour cream Tenochtitlán a spritz of lime
Spanish Conquest salsa Pancho iceberg lettuce stereotypes War on
Drugs jalapeños La Reforma black olives walls José María Morelos
cheddar cheese crammed into an edible shell and that's the beauty
nothing is left behind you can devour the whole goddamn thing.

PATHOLOGY OF VIOLENCE

Now

from a distance
mostly

drones hover
over every hovel and house

internet adversaries
portend each other's ruin

it's what makes us human
isn't it

this compulsion
to prove our permanence

and maybe violence
proves it more compellingly
than paintings

or poems

it burgeons

fist into spear into bow
into bomb

though we've heard
the tiny voices
buried beneath the rubble

though we've seen
arms flailing
from high windows

though we want better
for ourselves

and each other

there is another voice

that says the world
bends

around a blade
around a bullet

and where did I learn
as a child

to make a gun
of my hand

point my finger at the moon
and fire

and why is part of me
still waiting

for it to sputter from the sky

like a balloon filled
between god's puckered lips

suddenly let go?

POST-RACIAL

Walking meditation is first and foremost a practice to bring body and mind together peacefully.
— THÍCH NHẤT HẠNH

But what if I should discover that…the poorest of all the beggars, the most impudent of all the offenders, the very enemy himself— that these are within me…what then?
— CARL JUNG

I shorten my stride,
focus on my breath—in, out,
deep, slow—trying to bring body
and mind together peacefully,
to imitate the tight-lipped monks
circling their ashrams,

but my mind
is less obedient than my mutt,
part Rottweiler, part shepherd,
who—though agitated
by the chatty squirrels
that dart perilously close
as if to prove their bravery—
still stays by my side, wants them less
than he wants to hear *good boy*,
a few scratches under his chin.

So we walk—quiet, conflicted—

the sky darkens,
squirrels retreat to their nests,

and we find ourselves
under the graffitied bridge
most people avoid when, suddenly,
another set of footfalls join mine,
distant innocuous echoes
at first, and then faster, louder,

until my fearful imagination
works itself into a lather,
all thoughts of peace and monks
immolated here on the sidewalk
and in this pile of ash
is my pride, which, until now,
had held my gaze forward,
so finally, I turn and lock eyes
with the hooded Black teenager
trailing some 15 feet behind,

and despite my indignation—
my sorrow for Black boys
that get profiled and harassed
for being hooded and Black—
despite it, I pick up the pace,
glance over my shoulder
every few steps, watch the distance between us
shrink, consider running, loosing
the dog, wonder for the millionth time
if the city is safe, if I need
a gun, and what I would do now
if I had one,

but when I turn again—
to confront him this time—
he nods then crosses over
to the other side of the street,
to my great relief

and shame.

Is this the terrible mercy
he's already learned
to show white people,

or has he considered
how this night
could end—flashing lights,
crying mothers, Tamir was murdered
just a few blocks from here—

or does his crossing
have nothing to do with me
or the stories I tell?

Walking is too slow—
I want to run
from the worst parts of myself
like my dog kicks away from me
in leashless dreams. I want to
chase down goodness and carry it softly back
between my sharp and treacherous teeth.

BAPTISM

We assumed
the world existed
to give us everything
we wanted
handsome amiable
half-men
my friend and I
sixteen
at the beach
with a couple of budding
beauties we
made our way
down the shoreline
to a desolate
stretch of sand
one girl slipped into the surf left
the other to fend
for herself and boys
being boys being wolves
we tried to coax
the straggler into taking off
her bikini top
she smiled resisted shyly
unconvincingly
we were encouraged
riffed off each other
like masterful musicians
a serenade of appeals
and assurances
until finally she reached
behind her back
and with one tug

her flawless sunlit body
two smug smiles
a few seconds of ogling
before she resituated herself
turned toward the water
and it wasn't until after
my friend and I recounted our victory
that I noticed she was crying
her hands shaking as she tried
to light a cigarette
and I was too surprised
and too ashamed
to apologize wondered
what wounds I'd ripped open
felt paths open up
before me the many selves
I'd have to drown
and I walked
into Lake Erie
its brown waves up to my neck
a child baptized
into the religion of men
and the damage we do.

FLIGHT

Even before I sit, I spot the Bible in her lap, the crucifix
pinned to her lapel, and I imagine her enormous frame planted
in a pew: she offers meaty-pawed peace-be-with-yous,
sings jowly hallelujahs, sways one bulbous arm
to the hymns, the heavens
as the other works a folded fan—a vain attempt
to slow the sweat meandering from her swollen face
to her already soaked stockings.

Her body fits there
in that vision
like it will never fit here
on this plane, where I carefully contort
to squeeze past her.

After I fish
my seatbelt from under her weight,
apologizing again and again,
she smiles and asks
if I'm a believer, and I say, *no,*
not really,
and she says, *what about him?*
pointing at her lapel,
and I say, *well, I think a man*
is rarely his story,
and she says, *what?*
and I say, *never mind.* Her hips engulf
the armrest and sandwich my thigh. I want to believe
truth is what happens
when we erase the boundaries
between bodies. I want to tell her

about the Egyptian god Horus—
how he was born of a virgin, walked on water,
was crucified, and resurrected himself
three days later. Or

how the Persians' Mithras rounded up
twelve disciples, multiplied fish, and turned water
into wine. But I suspect
these similarities will mean very little to her,
as her god now means something
resembling nothing
to me. We are the same

in our denial, I think,
and find myself
liking that thought—
the possibility of parallel lives
despite all objections,
the bodies we wake to.

I don't want to swap stories. I want to sit
in silence, her leg touching mine—that small,
strange comfort—and I'll say nothing

of the good people I've hurt
or of the many ways I've betrayed them. I won't tell her
how badly I want to be forgiven

for all the sins I don't believe in.

NOCTURNE INTERRUPTED

Take my word
that the prelude wasn't pretty. Having disappointed
    the woman I love
again, she said something a little too true
to which I said something a little too dismissive
to which she said something a little too cruel
to which I said something worse.

And then a long evening of drumming up pain,
    the cacophonous business
of assigning blame—trading I-remember-whens
and I'll-never-forgive-you-fors—from which, exhausted,

I've retreated—strung my guilt over my shoulder like an old guitar
and hauled it out into the night. Here are the usual
    accompaniments—
the damp grass, the spotlight of the moon. Cicadas chirp.
    Occasionally,
an owl moans. It's all a stage for sadness.

Then, suddenly, a soulful howl
from the adjacent yard, a magnificent solo that stretches on and on

until Larry, my lanky neighbor with the bad haircut,
joins his dog—a late-night walk, I presume, and smile,
thinking of these two as silhouettes beneath streetlights,

but instead of latching a leash, Larry lifts his leg high
then down on the pup's back, snarling, *Shut up! Shut the fuck up!*
The dog scampers away, tail between its legs,
and Larry stalks after it, kicks and slaps, and this goes on
    for an eternity

of a few seconds—the howl replaced
by terrified whimpers. And finally, when he's made his point,
my neighbor stomps back into the silent confines of his house
and slams the door.

Only then does the dog dare to lift his head, which he turns
in the direction of his owner, and stares after him,
longs for him.

Who among us wouldn't hop that fence
and cradle that dog until he fell quiet?

Who among us hasn't been that animal, instincts screaming *run!*
but staying, loving because we don't know any better?

NIGHTMARE ON ELM STREET

Though they're meant to be our protagonists
we detest these teenagers
who fall for the same tricks and traps
in every film
and because they keep coming back
dumber and hotter
decade after decade
with their perky breasts and discernible abs
and the way they throw themselves mercilessly
against one another
in backseats and on twin beds
and because they smoke cigarettes
and slug soda and beer
and because dialysis and diabetes
will never creep like Freddy
into their dreams.
Because they're always in love
and loneliness is as unimaginable
as feigning sleep
so the person next to you
will stop kissing your neck
though you still care for her
and he's still beautiful
or maybe you don't
and maybe he's not
or maybe the workday has emptied you
of desire for anything
but seven hours of silence
and maybe these are the words you say
that can't be forgiven. Curse the children
for not knowing
that if you live long enough

life is mostly washing dishes
and may they suffer
for not believing
that young love dies
when the first person
goes to college
and meets a sorority girl
who can put her legs behind her head
or the backup point guard with the bulging
biceps. Twelve bucks is a bargain
to see these brainless babes
pierced by pitchforks, their chiseled flanks flayed
and hung from hooks. It's because
their failures will never grind them
into something so small
that they'll go to the theater alone,
buy some popcorn, and sit in the glow
of another slasher reboot, trying to distract themselves
from their disappointing lives.
It's because they'll never rise
between slaughters
and walk out into the night
in a relatively safe neighborhood
on the west side of Cleveland
and sit on a bench
with a pen and some paper
and write this poem,
like I've been doing all this time,
trying to find a way to drag
my bloody heart home.

APARTMENT B

That she killed herself
isn't altogether extraordinary.
Everybody has somebody—
an uncle, a friend of a friend.
Nor will it give us
much pause

to learn that she did it
with a gun, though they say
women prefer pills
or a hot bath and a razor.
But look closer—

her boyfriend fumbles
with his keys, drops
an armful of groceries
onto the counter, calls out
her name once
or twice
as he slides the sweating milk

into the fridge. Maybe
he thinks
she's in the shower
or out for a walk,
but when he rounds the corner
into the living room

she's standing there
with a gun in her mouth.
Maybe it's his. Maybe he hurt her
so badly

that she needs him
to watch.

And he does.

After a few beers,
my new neighbor
tells me his saddest
story. And when he's through,
he stares into his drink,
suddenly ashamed
of his sincerity.
I don't ask him
to fill in the blanks.

I don't ask
what new world
he's inhabited since
or what he could've done
to deserve this.

I don't ask how, four years later,
he can still live
in the apartment
where it happened—
walking those halls, cooking
in that kitchen, and,

I imagine, scrubbing
and scrubbing the floor.

SUICIDE

Sure
there are reasons to leave
a mother lights a cigarette
with her kid in the backseat
the ice caps melt
and hardly anyone bats an eye
much less considers the carpool lane
or public transit or the 10-speed
buried in the basement
and even the patch of weeds
some generous souls
call a park
is being paved over
by fat-pocketed colonizers
who have never rolled in the grass
or pondered the miracle of photosynthesis
who think the neighborhood
has *charm*
and so construction crews roll in
and condos and coffee shops
and rent go up
and the locals are forced
to the outskirts of town
and here
at the nexus of this exodus
in the twilight
between day and night
between before and after
another unarmed Black man
is shot by the cops
reaching for his cell phone
the Black man

it sometimes seems
an endangered species
like the snow leopard and giant panda
the blue whale and sea otter
like the tiger and readers of poetry
most of whom
will never pay off their student loans
especially if they're women
making 80 cents
to every dick's dollar
assuming they're lucky
enough to have escaped
the warzones
of their high schools
where another boy
pulls an AR-15 out of his locker
to turn classmates into meat
and childhood into a memory
and right now
as you read this poem
some misguided sap
stumbles into the most hateful rooms
on the internet
and starts to strap dogma or patriotism or sadness
to his chest like a bomb
or forget the simile
he literally straps a bomb to his chest
and it would soften the blow
if we could imagine these horrors
as aberrations
but we know they're mechanizations
of the institutions that support them
fear packaged with gun powder
and peddled by the NRA
and ISIS alike
the defense fund funneled

into arms corporations
and offshore accounts
that can be traced back to lobbyists
and cousins of congressmen
and so swarms of drones
eviscerate those misguided saps
and maybe by accident
a mosque or hospital or school
and somewhere someone is crunching the numbers
of how many civilian casualties
is too many civilian casualties
but before we have a moment to consider
what any of this means or how to fix it
there's another ding from the darkness
of America's pocket
the daily deluge of bad news
delivered in real time
and maybe your complexion is such
that you can retrieve your phone
on any street corner
without fear of being cuffed
or clubbed or becoming the star
of a body-cam video
and so you thumb
through headlines
and then past them
to memes and viral videos
staring dumbly at the screen
which is our new state of being
and so it seems that progress
is a wave
that has crashed down
on itself
tyrants reborn
bigotry re-elected
all the old hate

dug up and hung from flagpoles
and even
when you turn away
from the world
at the end of the day
you're still left with yourself
fatter than you remember
and you never visited Vienna
or climbed Kilimanjaro
and your job is one long sigh
and it's hard to stay in love or find joy
when you're dropping kids off
at soccer practice
or washing dishes caked
with day-old macaroni and cheese
and you are so tired
but the washer buzzes
in need of two arms
that used to be strong
to shovel the damp clothes
into the dryer

and sometimes
when you try to think of a reason to stay
you can't conjure
your children's awe
when they learn something new
or treasured breasts
unsheathed from their blouse
or your grandmother's pie crust
which by the grace of god
you've learned to recreate
and stuff with sun-kissed peaches
plucked from the neighbor's backyard
or how each change of season
seems like carefully curated mercy

as if someone knew we'd tire
of slathering sunscreen and shoveling snow
and raking leaves
and maybe under the weight
of your burden
you can't appreciate
the way traffic stops

for a funeral procession
and the faces around you
soften
into something like reverence
drivers and passengers
and pedestrians
suddenly grateful
perhaps
that they still have somewhere
to go
that their loved ones
are still in orbit
or else they remember
when they themselves
have had to take their place
in this slow-rolling dirge

and I wonder if you could see this now
if you would rise
open the rear door of the hearse
and put your hands up to stop the whole thing
if you would run to your wife and sons
and gather them into your arms
praising the grass and traffic and ice caps
or if you would turn away again
untouched
and continue to march forward
on the long and lonely path

you've chosen.

LONELINESS

Slinks to bed
like a frightened child
who's too old
to still believe
in monsters,
too old to still believe
his father can protect him
from the worst of it.
Maybe it's my fault
that I didn't teach him better,
didn't make him tougher,

but, regardless, I'm grateful
he shows up like this—
humbled, softened,
his sharp corners
sheared—that he never
became
or befriended
those kids
that we fear.

You know the ones.
They hide razors
in bottom drawers,
say things like
I hate you
and *I wish I was never born.*
Maybe their angst ends
there—a few slammed doors,
a broken phone.
Maybe they shed

their meanness
and thank you
once or twice
before your long,
last sleep.

Or maybe they
shoot their arms
full of poison
and when the veins
shrink and hide
they still find a way
between their fingers
and toes, which you remember
being so small
in a memory
that no longer feels
like yours.

Maybe you're lucky
and they only impale themselves
on their sadness
or maybe you're not
and they bully the new girl
into an eating disorder
or send siblings
through windshields
or pick up rifles
and march into cafeterias
or proms
to scythe classmates
as if they were fields of wheat.
What can you do
but love what's yours?

Remember,

this is a metaphor,
which doesn't mean
it isn't real. We're talking
about loneliness,
how it's swaddled
and entrusted to us,
and how you never really know

if it will say *please*
and *thank you*
and grow up
to meditate
and learn from its mistakes,

or if it'll litter and kick the cat
and carve itself up,
breaking your heart.
Imagine feeling
like it can't be fixed—

loneliness born
with balled-up fists
it'll carry through all its days,
unable to appreciate

how the hearts swells
at some small kindness
or a friend's good news or the birds
or the moon when it spreads its pasty shadow
on the bedroom floor,

where my loneliness often patters
its tiny feet, all in all a sweet kid,
a little too sensitive, sure,
wanting me to explain
every ache and pain,

where he came from
and what went wrong,

and sometimes I let him crawl
under the covers
and he falls asleep in my arms,
and other times I carry him
back to his room.
Tell me a story, he says.
I only know one, I say.
Tell me again, he says.
And I do.

II

❧

i saw a small moon rise
from the breast of a woman
lying in a hospital hall
and I saw that the moon was me
and I saw that the punctured bag
of a woman body was me
and i saw you sad there in the lobby
waiting to visit and I wanted
to sing to you
go home
i am waiting for you there

—LUCILLE CLIFTON

DIPTYCH

On the path where I walk my dog
a dead cardinal is becoming

        my mother

            has returned
      to the same hospital

      where twenty years ago
           chemo almost killed her
      before the cancer could

      so she stands
           petrified
      as patients

   and passersby
tiptoe around

the bird's remains

     glued to the concrete

        outside oncology

      where not even a new coat of paint
           can stop her body's remembering

      the surge of vomit

      she deposits
           near the entryway

fading

      a little more each day

as ants

    haul the carrion away

  until all that's left
      is an outline

      a shadow
        you could walk right by

  but on my knees
    I can still see

  the beak turned to the side
wings spread wide

        the occasional smile

      doing better
    at least

      than her friend
      the one who didn't make it

        who lost his meals when he saw nurses
        at the grocery store or walking *their* dogs

    but soon

      even I won't be able to recognize her
flying against the gritty sidewalk

    so not of this world

that my dog no longer sniffs
where there used to be feathers
    and bones

        and

            what I want to know is
          will I ever be able to think of her

as she was

    whole
          and unafraid

    soaring?

SEASONS

She starts chemo
in the summer.
You sweep up her hair
and take it outside.
Let it go in the wind.
Straighten her wig.
Tell her she looks beautiful
and you both stand awhile
with the lie
until she loses the strength
to stand. And then you sit
with the sadness,
holding her hand.

Come fall,
the doctors decide
to slice her open.
To pull out the polluted
organs. She's so scared
when they wheel her away
that she shakes uncontrollably.

The surgery takes six hours.
You stare at the clock.
Finally, the pager goes off
and you have never been
so thankful.
They sew her up.
Bring her to a room.

You sit next to her
and watch her breathe.

She wakes somehow
with a small smile. A miracle.
You take her home.
Clean the staples and stitches,
a zipper splitting her
right down the middle.

She gets stronger.

For a couple weeks,
she's cured.
Singing Joplin.
Scrambling eggs.
Holding your arm
on slow walks
around the block.
Talking spring.

But the pain comes back.
Worse than before.
The winter clouds.

It'll snow soon, she says,
looking out the window.
And she's right.
It won't take long
for the seams to burst.

For all that beauty
to come tumbling out.

IT TOOK SEVEN DAYS FOR MY MOTHER TO DIE

I.

I answer the phone
it takes a moment
for my father to gather himself
on the other end of the line
and so I know
even before he says *bad news*

the oncologist
so full of promise
Plan Bs Plan Cs
all the way down the alphabet
now says my mother is too weak
for any more treatment
nothing left to be done

I ask how long
Dad sighs
says *a couple weeks*
maybe a couple months
I hear Mom in the background
so tired so brave
say *it could be a couple days*
almost hopeful

I want to go to her
but they ask for one last night
just the two of them
before the dying begins in earnest

I walk the city for hours
zip my coat to my chin
watch my breath disappear
into the night
the cold numbs fingers and toes
creeping
toward the center of me

II.

I drive the hour to my parents' house
the house where I grew up
sit in the driveway
wonder what I can possibly say

I give up go inside
and find her in the recliner
my father bought
when she started to struggle
to get in and out of bed

her eyes are closed asleep
or maybe meditating
a practice she picked up
these past few months
when the pain got to be too much

her eyes are closed
asleep or meditating
I stand on the precipice of the room
and consider a third option

but her eyes flutter open
and I think we have not been
mother and son more completely

since the day I was born
she shrugs as if to say *we tried*
and then smiles
and then realizes she's smiling
and stops

I sit next to her and hold her hand
as I've done almost every weekend
for the past eight months
I tell her again how sorry I am
she squeezes my hand tighter and says

she wants to say what she has to say
and then she needs to focus
I say okay
she says the funeral should be simple
asks me to write the eulogy
makes me promise to make peace with my sister
and keep my father off the roof
look after them both she says
and asks that this be the end of tears and goodbyes
since crying sends her heaving
into empty coffee cans
stashed all over the house

I tell her I love her
she breathes for a long time
says *there was never any doubt*
we sit like that
until evening comes
and with it

the hospice team
who knock and enter and shake hands
so gently the dog doesn't even lift his head
we make plans to *manage her journey*

I start to understand

III.

This is the last day she'll speak
in full coherent sentences
though she stops halfway through
a thought
and for so long
I wonder if anything will follow

she hasn't eaten in two days
except for a little ice cream
from the pint I brought her
butter pecan
her favorite

which she works around
her sore-filled mouth for a while
swallows
looks at me and says *it's good*
though a spoonful is all she can manage
and I won't realize until later
that she does this for me

IV.

My sister comes home without her husband
or children it's the four of us again
five
if you count the baby to be born
a few months from now
the grandchild Mom will never meet

we sit next to her
and feed her pills one for pain
which makes her restless
one for insomnia which causes cramps
one relaxant which clouds her thoughts
we bring her fresh glasses of water
to wash them down
take turns retreating to the kitchen
to shuffle around old pizza boxes
and casseroles we talk to the on-duty nurse
update relatives try to read
and watch TV
mostly Mom sleeps
between moans and whimpers
we look at her we look at each other
we pretend we aren't waiting

V.

She's too weak now
to hold her head up
it lolls around
we try to get her into the hospital bed
hospice delivered but she looks us
in the eyes and sets her jaw
drifts off again

we prop her up with pillows
try to make her more comfortable
to battle the nerve pain
blazing through her limbs
we give her too many pills
she can no longer swallow
so we crush them up
mix them with a little water

and use what looks like a tiny turkey baster
to shoot the concoction into her cheek
where it dissolves
sometimes she tries to spit it out
so we have to hold her mouth shut for a second
she sleeps all day
then suddenly hoarse from not drinking
she whispers *take me to bed*
so I can die

we stand her up
help her to the bedroom
tuck her in
she weighs almost nothing
my father looks shocked
he takes off his socks gets into bed
and cradles her

my sister and I say goodbye
tell her we love her over and over
kiss her forehead
and move upstairs
to wait in different rooms

I think about what my mother said
after she was diagnosed
that she was less afraid of dying
than of being in pain
which she remembered so well
from her first bout with cancer
a couple decades ago

I think about what she said
a few months later
that each morning she couldn't imagine
suffering through another day

until she made it into bed with my father
and he held her like he's done
for the past thirty-three years
and then she thought she had the strength
to do it all again

and I picture them together
down there
wrapped up for the last time

VI.

Around 4 a.m. I hear rustling
Dad speaking softly
unmistakably
to Mom
she's still alive
I'm equal parts relieved
and horrified

I go downstairs
we help her
to the bathroom
finally convince her
to get into the hospital bed
adjust it so she's sitting up

Heidi
our regular nurse
arrives at 7:30
tells us we're not there yet
but close
we leave the room
so she can give Mom a sponge bath

and insert a catheter
we understand now what Mom already knew
that she'll never leave this bed alive

never get up
and power walk around town
waving at every passerby
never spot spring's first cardinal
or deliver one of her long drawn-out jokes
never retire or hold her grandchildren
or feel the grass under her feet
never order an ice cream cone
or pick up the phone to tell us
the exact thing we need to hear
never stand at the stove
which she did even when she was sick
leaning on her walker with one hand
stirring spaghetti sauce with the other

now there's only the landscape
behind her eyelids
where she remains throughout the day
even when we think
to roll the bed near the window
so she can see the birds
that have arrived miraculously
in late November to feast at her feeder
a strange sign we think
but when she finally does open her eyes
the birds have flown off to wherever they go
power line or nest or somewhere down south
gone maybe for good
maybe a sign after all

early evening
we rouse her for more pills

she looks at me fevered and wide-eyed
asks *should I be mad at you?*
I'd hoped she'd been dreaming
of something kind and cliché
her wedding day
or departed loved ones
beckoning her home
that sort of thing
maybe some private memory she cherishes
that I'll never know
or any of the many mundane days
she spent with her family
which she treasured above all
she'd tell us even then
spoiling the levity
the easy rhythm of the afternoon
and we'd tease her for her sentimentality
which she smiled at
proud of her oversized heart

and how naïve to believe
she could find much comfort anywhere
that pain would spare sleep
or any part of her

no I don't think so
I say and she seems relieved
closes her eyes again
and we prepare for what will be
the worst night of our lives

my father and I take shifts
one of us at her side holding her hand
the other curled up on the couch
trying to steal a few minutes of sleep
also naïve

we listen to her breathe
the apnea especially cruel now
a cluster of uneven breaths
a shallow exhale and then nothing
and just when we're sure no more will follow
her body jerks into a desperate suck of air
as if she's drowning
over and over
and when the man holding her hand
can take no more we switch spots
try to muffle our crying in the darkness

VII.

This goes on for hours
until morning when incredibly
a half-sister not seen in years arrives
having driven seven hours
straight through the night
the house filling with ghosts
mercifully she takes our seat

I walk upstairs to the kitchen
slowly chew some Cheerios
though we ran out of milk days ago
I pour another bowl and chew slower
I know what's at the end of this chewing

my sister wakes
puts two slices of bread into the toaster
I swallow and head back downstairs
we're very close now Heidi says
and I hardly believe her
I've begun to think this will go on forever

Mom is slack-jawed head cocked to the left
the horrible gargled breathing
the breathing the breathing
like something inside of her wants out
I can't stop thinking about it
I could write ten more pages about it

Heidi says that as the body dies
it focuses all its energy
on the most important organs
as if on cue Mom's chest descends violently
this is it Heidi says and runs upstairs
to tell my sister

I rest my hand on Mom's left shoulder
my father holds her left hand
and my sisters mirror us on her right

is it over? my father sobs
she may take a couple more breaths Heidi says
and then she does and then she doesn't
and we don't need to ask
after the last one we know
we keep touching her
one of my tears falls into her hair

Heidi leaves the room
but none of us move
we sit together
a mismatched family
a family nonetheless
I look up and expect to see the birds
but they aren't here now either

I've never seen my father cry before this week
but this is something new

a guttural despair I let myself
follow as I always have
his example

after what could be minutes or hours
Heidi comes back tells us
that when we're ready
she'll clean Mom up and get her dressed
tasks are assigned

we trail off one by one
sisters to Mom's closet to pick an outfit
my father and I to the kitchen
where uncles and aunts have materialized
we give hugs pass out cups of coffee
I think Mom would've liked this otherwise
we shake our heads take turns saying
I can't believe it and *she deserved better*
when I go to refill someone's coffee
I notice two burnt slices of toast
still in the toaster the world split
into *before* and *after*

Heidi appears and says Mom is ready
we file downstairs
she is dressed sunken and pale
a hand towel rolled under her chin
to keep her mouth closed Heidi explains
and I look at her confused
she pantomimes lifting her lower jaw
and I feel something inside of me shift
and sink

sometime later
the funeral director shows up
with one other person

it's the day before Thanksgiving

no one else in the office
so it's up to the men in the house
to roll Mom onto her side
slide a sheet beneath her
lift her into the body bag
and carry her up the stairs
navigating two sharp turns
as if she were a piece of furniture

my uncles and father with their bad hips
shoulders and knees and me
with my broken heart
we carry her outside to the stretcher
and they roll her away to be cremated

a year ago
she had no idea what lurked inside of her
but still liked to say *be good to each other*
appreciate it
it goes so fast
sometimes we'd smirk shake our heads
as if to say *that's Mom*
and other times it rang true
and we'd look at each other
much like we're doing now
in the cold air trying to understand
what time makes of us

we return inside
sit with the funeral director to draft
an obituary
she pulls out a pen
opens to a fresh page in her notebook
asks *where did she work?*

who did she love?
what did she do for fun?

STAGES

Before you died
denial
seemed absurd

how could I
not be consumed
like Jonah
by the whale
and come to live
in the belly
of loss
lighting my one
candle

how could I refute
what would be so plain
and omnipresent
that all we've said
is all we'll ever say
and all we've done
all we'll ever do

how could I
mistake absence
for presence
fill the space
where your body had been

I didn't understand

but now I walk
into empty rooms

and think
where are you?
it's true
I can't believe it

I call the house
to hear your voice
on the answering machine
sometimes someone picks up
and I think it will be
you.

MY MOTHER PREPARES ME FOR HER DEATH

She'd give me the slip
in the toy department, a boy distracted
by swords and flashing lights and pogo sticks.
A few minutes would pass before I'd notice her hand was gone,
along with the rest of her, and I'd scamper aimlessly
from electronics to men's fashion to automotive,
the soles of my shoes leaving streaks of black like breadcrumbs.
Somewhere in that fluorescent abyss, a boy in a heap, *Mommy*
on the tip of his blubbering lips.

This is what it takes. Your legs have to fail.
Red eyes have to empty. You must come to terms
with the reality of loss. Only then
would my mother emerge from her hiding spot—
glide like Lazarus from the dressing room
or part the curtain of cardigans on the carousel—
where she'd been watching the whole time.

It's been twenty years since we played her game,
and I'd all but forgotten that boy. But today, as my dog
and I take a shortcut through a graveyard,
I find myself crouching behind a headstone.
When he realizes I've vanished, he lies down
as if he'll never move again, and I can sense
the weight of loss in him, the lightness in me.

I know this story begins with my mother.
I know it ends underground. I know
we're somewhere in between, waiting for that step into sunlight,
where, as if by magic, everything we love
will be given back.

FAMILY

Because my mother is dead
my father starts to tell stories
about his dead mother
and so we are
in our grief
almost brothers

tonight
one of my favorites
about the time
he and his friend
drunk
both home from college
went fishing
in the middle of the night
and hit the jackpot
caught 300 smelt
which they cleaned
and brought
to my grandmother
who in my imagination
takes the shape
of my mother
so alike they were
in their goodness

and right as I think it
my father says
sometimes I wonder
if I married my mom
which for some
may conjure Oedipus

but just makes me think
how lucky

to have found two women
in a lifetime
who would wake
at 3 a.m.
and amble into the kitchen
in their nightgowns
to fry fish after fish
as you and your buddy
get louder
drinking beer after beer
which you pad
with salted smelt
pulled straight from the oil

what wouldn't I give
to pull up a chair
next to my father
in that smoky kitchen
and crack open a cold one
laughing over our haul
and all the old stories
as our mothers stand
at the stove
looking over their shoulders
every so often
to smile at their sons.

LOSS

Because it's the first day of fall
I'm thrown headlong
into end-of-summer dramatics
walking the dog thinking
that life is a long rehearsal
for death a series of losses
leading to the singular loss

and in my despair
it seems suddenly necessary
to start to list the pain to come
family and friends whose passing
would gut me
and as I count distractedly
on fingers then toes

I walk into a low-hanging branch
which rakes me almost lovingly
across the face and I'm like
the student in the back of the classroom
with his head on his desk
startled awake by a question
to which he finally
finally knows the answer

and forget what *we* know
that this student's answer
is almost always
wrong and often even
incomprehensible
but what grace to sometimes stumble
into the peripheral foliage

of the lesson plan

like this branch
which I'm awed to see
has defied the season and sprung
a litter of buds
of which I pluck one
and move to place it on my tongue
an impulse that somewhere
has made Freud proud
but then I think no

the mouth so greedy
for air and water
and the lips of one another
but what about
my thrice broken nose
which like that student suddenly
asserts its strange utility

not for spring's flourish
or mama's pasta sauce or in defense
of the dank dumpster
behind my apartment building

but here for this bud
which is neither floral nor nostalgic
nor full of my neighbor's
cat's kitty litter but also
not entirely odorless
and so I split the struggling shoot
and sniff again at its faint
perfume

which I've spent most of my life
walking by

these small out-of-season miracles
that have been
sure I'll say it
right here under my nose
so prolific and ubiquitous
I've nearly forgotten
to mourn them.

FORESHADOW

Here we are in front of a sign claiming
The World's Largest Watermelons!
My mother and father wave, all three sisters
give me bunny ears, and I stare dumbly
into the camera. A gardener snaps our picture
and then we wander away from each other
to tend to our own wild patches of thought,

lost in those furrows
until my father bellows from the bottom
of the crate he's burrowed himself in,
heaving unworthy melons into a heap,

he rises,

tongue between his teeth, arms wrapped
around a behemoth, jungle green.
And then we're huddled in the kitchen—
my father smiles as he slides the knife
into the fruit, my mother wrings her hands,
two sisters hold out their plates,
and the third swings her soon-to-be aerated arm
over my shoulder. How anxious we are
to know if it tastes as good as it looks,

and then how its juice snakes across the counter
like all the sticky messy secrets we never learn
until the cutting has been done.

A LESSON IN ANNIHILATION

All water has a perfect memory and is forever trying to get back to
where it was.
              —Toni Morrison

And being mostly water, there is mutiny in our bodies.
    It wants out—
our wrists slashed and drained. Better yet, it wants us from the inside,
    says,

Swim until you can swim no longer. What we call
the urge to self-destruct is only this—a way back home, a gift

the giver wants back. See, it's water's voice sloshing around
in the murk we call *loneliness* and mistake as our own. What's a girl

to do? Tossed overboard. Drowning in the muddy depths
of her head. Perhaps you thought the bathtub romantic,

overkill a symptom of dedication. Handful of pills. Something sharp.
One can never be too careful. One can never outrun water,

though you tried, and once with me, your eyes
    in the rearview mirror,
scanning the empty street. Any moment, you thought,

the flood of grief would come growling out of the darkness
and pour through the broken windows. But your gaze settled
    with each state line,

and a slow inversion blossomed at the corners of your mouth. Then,
miles of cows. Tepid coffee and water-stained ceilings.

Of course we ended up at the ocean—sleeping on sand,
    swimming at sunrise.
Each time you dove underwater, I held my breath.
    Counted the seconds.

After three days, you had just enough money to get us back home—
what could we do but fill the tank, turn around, and face our fate?

I was grounded for two months and you were shipped off
to rehab. To everyone's surprise, you embraced therapy

and came back clear-eyed and calm. I was convinced your body
would forget its dissent, that the waves would ebb
    until they were silent.

But water's memory is insistent. It wasn't long
    before you filled the tub,
rattled those pills into your palm, and opened the dam

of your skin. You were emptied. And on the other side
of the locked door the firefighters hacked down,

it was me screaming your name. I spent my childhood
hiding razors, begging you to stick around.

I spent my childhood trying to convince you
that sadness wasn't in your blood. You spent yours

trying to see for yourself.

ASYLUM PASTORAL

At the abandoned Central State Sanitarium for the Insane in Milledgeville, Georgia

You can almost imagine
what it was like—
the dried-out fountain
come to life, rhododendrons
pruned down to size,
glinting glass windows
instead of two-by-fours
nailed akimbo.

Now,
the sidewalk knuckles,
puddles pool
on the ruined roof,
and ivy slithers wildly
down the spine
of the moldering
holding cells,
as if to defy
the precisely placed
magnolia, the petunia.
The whole site sags
into its sad history:
bloodletting, isolation therapy,
lobotomies—torture
disguised as treatment.

Once, there were clipped hedges,
the fountain babbled,

and the windows gleamed—
there was a kind of order here,
and how cruel
to surround anyone with beauty

and to demand sanity.

AUDIENCE

Winter's first snowfall
comes early
catches everybody
by surprise my dog
paws at a patch
in the park birds
voice displeasure
from trees lining
the sidewalk
and across the street
there's a family parents
with two young daughters
sandwiched
between them
all holding hands
their heads tipped back
tongues out
and then I see a woman
alone in her car
at a stoplight
and she's smiling too
watching the family
we're all smiling
me watching her
watching them
I imagine this
stretching on block
after block city
after city I look
around to see
who's watching me
but no one's there

the streets are otherwise
empty it will snow
for a long time.

WINTER

Today
sunlight in waves

the clouds part

and coalesce

and part again

I try to memorize
each moment

feel
each ray

that brief
shimmer

then
as it must

the warmth ebbs

light
like memory

and suddenly
I realize how far it's come

how improbable the journey.

MONOLOGUE, WITH DOG

Old friend,

we walk
these deserted city streets, quiet

but for the highway's
harmonious hum.

Out here
in the night,

we're usually contented,
usually calmed—

so what is it
inside of you

that suddenly tosses its head back
and empties its throat

into the sky,

though the moon is hidden
and most of your kind

folded at the foot
of some master's bed?

And tell me,
isn't this joy?

To call out
into darkness,

expecting silence,

and then to hear a voice
you remember,

as if from a dream,

howl back?

KAYAKING, EARLY MORNING

Surely, if god exists,
he'll choose now to speak with me.
Now being the perfect time,
considering just ahead on the river
there is the crane's cadence—
how it weaves in and out of the sunlight
piercing the trees, how the oaks' leaves
drift from branches
to settle on water, sending ripples
into orbit—an echo to fall's arrival.

It's no secret
that I'm too easily distracted
by beauty. Con men can smell me—
sell me anything if it's shiny
and symmetrical.

So, of course these solitary trips downriver
leave me vulnerable.
And if god dropped by
to talk to me, man to man,
hombre a hombre,
forfeiting his guises of burning bushes
and thunder and lightning,
I'd probably forget myself
and firmly shake his hand—even thank him,
perhaps, for the birds,
all that business with the sun.

I wouldn't ask
about war, racism, or natural disasters,
and I certainly wouldn't inquire

about Mom's recurring cancer
or blue-faced overdosed sisters.

With so much sleight-of-hand splendor,
he could come and he could go,
and no one could ever say he didn't give
at least one of us a chance to understand
this misery, this bewildering beauty.

FOUND MANTRA IN THE FROZEN FOOD AISLE

The woman lets go of the freezer door
at the exact moment her toddler lunges
for a box of fudgsicles, his greedy hand outstretched
like Michelangelo's Adam reaches eternally
for god—the pink stubs of what will become
a man's fingers, hands that will someday search
for something to cling to and call holy.

And when the door inevitably swings shut
across his soft, unblemished knuckles, he screams
as if to mourn yet another crumb of innocence

snatched. His mother wraps him up in her arms,
brushes his hand against her cheek, presses
each finger to her lips. She shushes him softly, sweetly.

But the child is inconsolable. He does not know yet
that the pain will end. He doesn't know the pain

will end.

SOMEDAY, YOU TOO WILL BE
ON HOLD WITH THE INSURANCE
COMPANY

For Aria, my niece, on her first birthday

Someday, you too will be on hold with the insurance company,
and when Rebecca—the operator who's already mumbled
her way through three department transfers—condemns you
to another fifteen minutes of that soul-shattering synth music,
    remember me

already an hour late for your first birthday party, and later still
after stumbling through yet another poem. In this life,
    you must say you're sorry
the best way you know how. Someday, darling, you will hurt—
a bone will need reset, a tooth drilled—and when Rebecca,
with her loose command of the English language, finally delivers
    some good news,
which you'll ask her to repeat, just to be sure, her voice will be that
of an angel. Trust me.

And though I sometimes wish I might become the type of uncle
who detects concerning clicks in your car's crankshaft
or gifts you pepper spray for your birthday
or interrogates boyfriends or girlfriends under a hot lamp,
    I know I won't
be able to protect you, especially from what you love.
    I'll never understand
what to do with pain, but I can tell you that on the other side of it

there's this:

a short drive to a baby born in the shadow of Halloween.
    How certain we'll be
that we regret nothing
when you emerge joyous from your slice of cake,
        slathered in frosting
and speckled with crumbs. And later, after a wet rag and some tears,

your parents will unveil your newest party trick—
        when they say, *Zombie baby*,
you, with your mostly toothless mouth, will groan, *Arrrrrrrgggg*,
as if undead, as if hungry for brains,
though you can't even say my name.

Make no mistake—it will be hard at times
to live. Years from now,
you may doubt that it's you in those pictures, a smiling pudge
topped with a tuft of hair. But you were there. I know. I held you
        in my arms.

Baby girl, do better than any of us. Be kind.
    Though I may deserve it—
perpetually late, perpetually failing
the ones I love—do not eat these brains. Believe me,
        they're mostly mush anyway,
but they're all I have to give, and there's still so much
I need to tell you.

REVELATION

If there's one thing
my father tried to teach me

it's that there's a right way

to load the dishwasher

a right way
to clean the toilet bowl
mow the lawn
change a tire
build a fire

and though I could never
make a religion
out of landscaping or perfectly placed
plates

I spent years thinking
I only had two options

right and good
or wrong and bad

and I wanted to be good
wanted to be right

which of course
meant righteous

my whole life
I've been looking for something solid

a straight line I could follow
all the way through

I thought I'd find it
if I read the right books

met the right people

a code
a key that would unlock
everything else

there were bits and pieces
everywhere

but I couldn't make them fit

I tried to write my way
toward it

an incantation
a set of instructions

I still don't even know what *it*
is

look
I filled up an entire book

and this is what it took
to start to hear the music
in my mistakes

my hands in the sink
washing the dish
that didn't come clean

my dog perched
in the patch of grass
higher than the rest

my feet carrying me away
from the car on the jack

and these poems
which I hoped might reveal
the wisdom I lack

well
they keep bending
into questions

forgive me
I can't stop believing

there's a right answer
that you might have it

think of the coffee-stained cup
the casserole-caked pan
the fork and the space between prongs

think of how they're rolled into their dark cave
and if properly arranged

how they come out new

that's what I want for you
from you

I understand so little

and I fear
and pray

that I'll have to do this forever
to ever say what I'm supposed to say

there are so many words
so many signs
so many ways
to beg.

PSALM I

I've met a woman
who really loves trees. Perhaps
you think that adverb lazy, but I'm here
to tell you that I'm a man
who loves trees. I've learned their names:

hawthorn, honey locust, slippery elm. Some are deciduous
and some are coniferous, and, even more, I love
the way that sounds. *Deciduous. Coniferous.*

But I don't *really* love trees. Or the birds
that make homes in the nooks of their branches.
Whole ecosystems are born and die
without my adverbial love. Stars explode.
Planets vanish. Chunks of night sky are swallowed
and my inexplicable heart keeps beating.

Really, I'm hung up on words, my old dog Rufio,
and the pillow of that woman's ass
where I rest my head as we lie in the grass—friends,
this is where I want to nest, live,
and die. What I mean to say is: there is so little time

and so much to worship. That we have to choose
is the only tragedy. But there are enough of us
on this glossy planet to love everything well.

Will we ever say the right names? Will we ever sing
their litany? Is it too sudden to start here,

now?

COMMUNION

No matter the season
I bike to work
fire up my lungs and legs
like a jalopy sputtering to life
all clatter and clank
until I hit smooth pavement
and higher gears greedy
to gulp the cool air
Lake Erie pitches inland
becoming almost
a child again
picking up speed
feeling fast and free
and if this sounds romantic
that's because it is
every morning I wake panicked
certain that some disaster awaits
until I swing one leg
over the crossbar
grip the handles
push off and remember
wind sunlight birds trees
the world settling
into its familiar rhythms
the miracle of the mundane
romantic yes but also
parking downtown
is fifteen bucks a pop
and the traffic on Carnegie
enough to transform
morning anxiety into something
truly sinister

so I ride
fortunate that years ago
during a particularly savage
thunderstorm
security waved me
into the executive garage
though clearly I was
and am
a low-level lackey
but I kept showing up
and they kept waving me in
smiling less and less
tolerating me as if a stray
they fed one too many times
and now feel responsible for
and every morning we nod
as if to affirm our unspoken agreement
that if I don't chew through any wires
or shit in the house
they won't chase me away
with a broom

though come winter
they're welcoming again
and despite record high
temperatures
a soupy Christmas
and light-jacket New Year
February suddenly decides
to show its mettle
dumps two feet of snow
that I slog through to the office
where the valet line has slowed
and snakes out into the street
and the big wigs look at me
quizzically from their heated

leather bucket seats
in their fuel-inefficient cars and I
the human-shaped icicle
on wheels look back
just as quizzically and truly
we are strangers
maybe even
I often think
enemies

but today
I'm too exhausted
too in love
with the chill in my bones
to hate
and I wish
we could stay here like this
studying each other
until our frigid differences thawed
until we acknowledged
all the lies we tell ourselves
about ourselves about the other
and we'd abandon
our cars bikes buildings
fax machines political affiliations
and walk hand in hand
into the formidable
and magnificent seasons
all of us in our loin cloths
hunting gathering building fires
worshipping the earth
sea and stars feeding each other
berries from our stained
and calloused hands.

T.J. SANDELLA is the author of *Ways to Beg*, his debut collection, which was a finalist or semi-finalist for several awards, including the Miller Williams Poetry Prize, the Brittingham & Felix Pollak Prizes, and the Crab Orchard First Book Award. Selected by Dorianne Laux for inclusion in the *Best New Poets* anthology, he is the recipient of an Elinor Benedict Prize for Poetry (selected by Aimee Nezhukumatathil), a William Matthews Poetry Prize (selected by Billy Collins), two Academy of American Poets Prizes, and two pushcart prize nominations. He lives in Cleveland, Ohio.